Your future starts now!

www.futuresmartminds.com

Welcome to the world of **STEM** innovation, **Future Engineers**! We are thrilled that you've chosen "**Future Engineer**" as your gateway to an exciting journey into the world of engineering and discovery. At **FutureSmartMinds**, we are passionate about nurturing young minds and fostering a deep love for **STEM** learning. Your purchase of "**Future Engineer**" not only empowers your child with hands-on engineering experiments but also supports our mission of inspiring the engineers and inventors of tomorrow.

Your feedback is invaluable to us. If "**Future Engineer**" has kindled the spirit of innovation in your young engineer or brought educational joy to your family, please consider sharing your thoughts on Amazon. Your review will help other parents and aspiring engineers explore the wonders within these pages.

Scan to Rate Us on Amazon

Thank you for being part of our **STEM** family, and here's to a future filled with endless possibilities and innovative minds!

Warm regards,

The FutureSmartMinds Team

www.futuresmartminds.com

Email: FutureSmartMindsKids@gmail.com

 @futuresmartminds

 @futuresmartminds

 @futuresmartminds

Scan to visit our website

Content	Page

Content	Page

What is Engineering?

Science and engineering often intersect, as they both utilize similar theories and aim to enhance human life. While science primarily delves into understanding the 'why' behind natural phenomena – like why objects are drawn towards the Earth – engineering applies these scientific principles to practical uses. A perfect example of this application is how engineers use the concept of gravity in the design and functionality of rockets.

Therefore, scientists develop theories regarding natural phenomena and provide proof for their theories. Engineers use these theories and apply them to solve real-life problems.

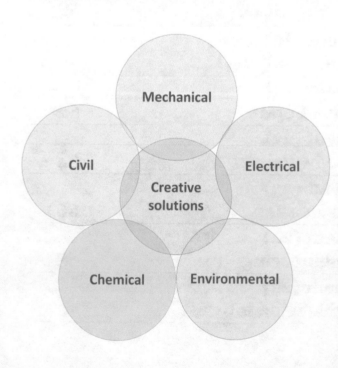

The goal of an **engineer** is to **design and implement solutions** that solve social, economic, and environmental problems. It usually takes different branches of engineering, such as **mechanical, electrical, civil, chemical, and environmental**, to work together to develop a solution. Each branch participates in a design and implementation process, including creative solutions that make people's lives more comfortable and transform the world into a better place.

Engineers follow a series of steps to find a solution for a problem; these steps include **identifying the problem, brainstorming solutions, selecting a solution, designing and testing the solution, and improving the design**.

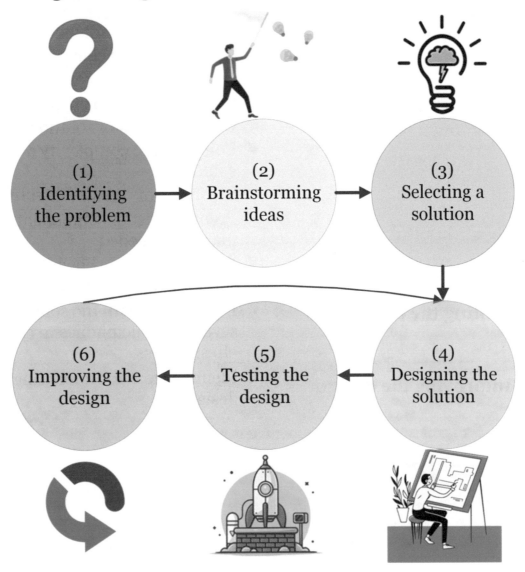

For example, suppose an engineer is looking into ways to solve issues related to **mobile phone devices**. The engineer would investigate common problems users encounter while using their mobile phones and try to design solutions that solve their problems. Let's look at how the engineer can follow the **engineering process** steps to accomplish the task:

Engineering process	Example
(1) Identifying the problem	✔ Problem: mobile phone battery runs out of charge quickly
(2) Brainstorming ideas	✔ Create a long-lasting battery ✔ Create a mobile charger ✔ Improve mobile usage
(3) Selecting a solution	✔ Compare solutions feasibility ✔ Compare costs of solutions ✔ Compare the complexity of solutions ✔ Select the most suitable solution
(4) Designing the solution	✔ Prepare a list of components and materials needed ✔ Draw a diagram showing how the components are connected
(5) Testing the design	✔ Experiment with the solution on several mobile phones to check its effectiveness
(6) Improving the design	✔ Identify areas for improving the design

Fun Facts: Engineering

The word "**engineer**" is derived from the Latin word "**Ingenium**," which means native talent. The first engineer is believed to be Imhotep, who lived in Egypt around 2700 B.C. He played the leading role in designing and building the first pyramids in Egypt.

The first females to receive an engineering degree were **Elisa Zamfirescu and Nina Graham in 1912**. Eliza received her degree from the Royal Academy of Technology Berlin, and Nina received her degree from the University of Liverpool.

The most famous engineers who played a significant role in the development of the world:

- **Thomas Edison,** who invented the lightbulb and motion picture camera
- **Nikola Tesla** played a crucial role in inventing the radio, the X-ray machine, and induction motors
- The **Wright Brothers,** who created the first powered airplane

(1) Air-powered fast car

Get ready to race into the world of engineering with your very own air-powered fast car! Have you ever wondered how you can harness the power of the air? Let's build a super cool car that zooms using nothing but a balloon! You'll craft a car body, add wheels, and connect the axles. Then, you'll use a balloon to send your car flying across the room! So gather your household tools, and let's engineer some fun – your balloon-powered car awaits its first thrilling ride!

Concepts: Air pressure, potential energy, kinetic energy, Newton's third law of motion.

Material

- Plastic bottle
- 4 plastic bottle caps
- 1 wooden skewer
- 2 straws
- Balloon
- Tape
- Scissors

Instructions

(1) Cut one of the straws into two equal parts → **(2)** Tape the two halves of the straw to one side of the bottle *(look at illustration 1)* → **(3)** Cut the wooden skewer into two equal parts

(4) Insert the two pieces of the wooden skewer into the two halves of the straw

(5) Make sure that the skewer extends out of the straw from both sides. These skewers with straw sleeve will act as car axles

(6) Use the scissors to cut cross-shaped holes in the centre of the 4 bottle caps

(7) Insert the ends of the wooden skewer into the holes in the 4 caps to create the car wheels

(8) Place the car on a flat surface and push it forward and backward to check if the car rolls smoothly

(9) If the car does not roll smoothly, check if the axles are parallel to each other, the holes in the caps are centred, and the straws are well taped to the bottle

(10) Place the neck of the balloon around one end of the 2nd straw. Tape them tightly to prevent any air leakage

(11) Use the scissors to cut a hole in the top of the plastic bottle. Make sure that the hole is around the size of the straw

(12) Push the free end of the 2nd straw through the hole and out the bottle's mouth. Tape the straw to the bottle tightly

(13) Blow through the free end of the straw to inflate the balloon. Place your finger over the tip of the straw to trap the air

(14) Place the car on a flat surface and remove your finger to release the trapped air

(15) Watch your car goes fast on the flat surface and think of ways to make it goes faster

Illustrations

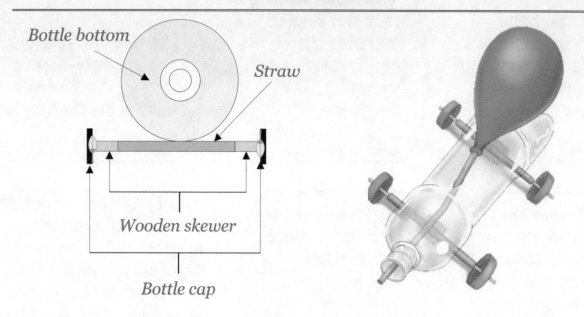

Bottle bottom

Straw

Wooden skewer

Bottle cap

How it works

🔧 Your air-powered fast car is an excellent example of **Newton's third law of motion**, which says that "for every action, there is an equal and opposite reaction."

💡 When you blow up a balloon, you increase the air pressure inside the balloon, which starts to stretch out the rubber surface of the balloon. The **air pressure** held inside the balloon and the stretched rubber surface of the balloon represent **potential energy** waiting to be released or transformed.

☝ When you remove your finger from the straw's tip, the balloon's stretched rubber surface contracts and starts to rapidly squeeze out the trapped air inside the balloon, converting the stored **potential energy** into **kinetic energy**.

🚗 **Zoom Forward**: With the air escaping backwards, there's an opposite reaction force that **propels the balloon** (and the car) forward - this is kinetic energy in motion.

⚡ **Energy Transformation**: The process showcases potential energy (stored energy) transforming into kinetic energy (energy of motion), resulting in the thrilling dash of your fast car.

As per **Newton's third law of motion**, when the air is squeezed out of the balloon rapidly towards the back, a reaction force pushes the balloon forward, causing your fast car to accelerate forward.

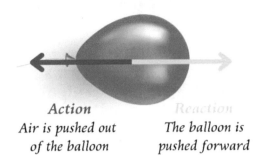

Action
Air is pushed out of the balloon

Reaction
The balloon is pushed forward

Troubleshooting

Engineering projects usually involve **trials, redesign, and improvement** to achieve great results. Iteration is part of any engineering project. Here is a list of possible faults you may encounter as you test your air-powered fast car and how to address them:

	Fault	*Solution*
1	The car does not move at all	✿ Check for stuck wheels ✿ Check if the tape is tight enough ✿ Make sure the inflated balloon is not touching the floor ✿ If the plastic bottle is heavy, try a lighter bottle
2	The balloon won't hold air	✿ If the balloon is broken, replace it with a new one ✿ Check the tape tightness around the straw and add more tape if necessary
3	The car moves slowly or turns to one side	✿ Check if the wheels or axles are crooked or bent to one side. ✿ Check if the bottle is in the centre and the wheels are parallel and centred

(2) Instant ice sculpture

Prepare to be amazed as you transform water into ice like magic with our 'Instant ice sculpture' experiment! By exploring the cool science of heat transfer, you'll learn how to supercool water and create ice in the blink of an eye. The secret lies in chilling the water just to the brink of freezing, where it hovers between liquid and solid. With just a simple pour, you'll witness a frosty wonder, turning water into ice sculptures right in your own hands. Let's uncover the icy point where water takes a whole new form!

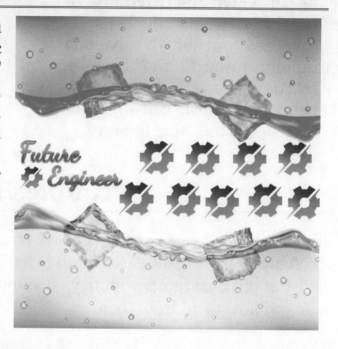

Concepts: Thermodynamics, heat transfer, snap freeze, crystallization

Material

- Water bottles
- Ice cubes
- Freezer
- Small bowl
- Towels

Instructions

(1) Place a few water bottles in the freezer for 2 hours, lay them flat on their sides

(2) Check the water bottles exactly after 2 hours. Did they start to harden?

Yes → Remove the bottles from the freezer

No → Return the bottles back in the freezer and check every 5 minutes

(3) Take the bottles out upon completion and place them on a flat surface. Place a towel underneath the bottles

(4) Place an ice cube in a small bowl and start pouring one of the water bottles on the ice cube

(5) Watch the water turn into ice as it touches the ice cube. Continue pouring the water on the ice to create an ice sculpture

How it works

❄ **Supercooled State**: The water was supercooled – chilled below freezing without turning to ice.

🌡 **Balancing Act**: This delicate balance kept the water liquid despite being cold enough to freeze.

🔍 **Crystal Formation**: Freezing water forms minute ice crystals, the building blocks of ice.

🧬 **Crystallization Chain Reaction**: These initial crystals trigger a rapid chain reaction called crystallization.

🧊 **Catalyst Ice Cube**: Pouring this supercooled water onto an ice cube sparks instant crystal growth, turning the water to ice before your eyes.

🧊 **Pure Water Phenomenon**: Purified water can stay liquid below 0 °C (32 °F) as it requires impurities to form ice crystals; introducing an ice cube provides the necessary surface for crystallization to commence.

Explore

Experiment with varying water temperatures: First, try supercooling water that has been heated before freezing. Observe and note the time difference between hot water reaching a supercooled state and water at room temperature. Does the initial temperature affect the rate of supercooling?

(3) Egyptian Screw Pump

Travel back to ancient times with the 'Egyptian Screw Pump' experiment! Over two millennia ago, ingenious Egyptians devised a pump, known as the screw pump, to raise water from the life-giving Nile River. This early pump represented a significant advancement in engineering, and its design was so successful that it caught the attention of Archimedes during his studies in Egypt.

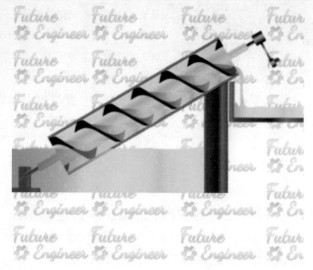

Archimedes brought this clever mechanism to Greece, where it continued to spread in use. With simple turns by hand, this device could transport water from low ground to high, changing the course of irrigation and civilization. Now it's your turn to build and operate a model of this historic pump with everyday materials!

Concepts: Screw, pump, slope, rotation, flow rate

Material

- 1-litre plastic bottle
- 5 ft (1.5 m) of plastic tubing, ¼-inch (6.4 mm) diameter
- 2 bowls
- Duct tape
- Food colouring
- Plastic sheeting

Instructions

(1) Tape one end of the plastic tubing onto one end of the bottle using duct tape. Leave about 1 cm hanging over the end

(2) Wrap the plastic tubing around the bottle in a spiral way at equal spaces until you reach the other end of the bottle. Leave about 1 cm hanging over the end

(3) Use pieces of duct tape to tape down the tubing on the bottle at each round and at the hanging ends of the plastic tubing

(4) Make sure that there is about 1 cm of tubing hanging off both ends of the bottle

(5) Pour one cup of water in one of the bowls and mix it with a few drops of water colouring

(6) Place the other empty bowl on an elevated surface. You may place the bowl on a book to raise it up

(7) Place one end of the bottle in the coloured water bowl with the other end resting on the higher empty bowl

(8) Make sure that the hanging tube at the bottle end is immersed into the coloured water and start turning the bottle slowly

(9) Continue turning the bottle and watch the coloured water as it goes into the tube all the way up and falls into the empty bowl

Experimental Iterations

Iterations are part of every single engineering project. You could end up with several trials before the experiment works out. Note the following design criteria and record the results of your iterations:

Slope

The slope of the screw pump determines the quantity of water raised by the pump and the time it takes to pump it. This is known as the water flow rate, measured in gallons per minute (gpm) or litres per second (l/s).

You can control the slope by adjusting the height between the coloured water bowl and the empty bowl. Start with raising the empty bowl level 1 inch above the coloured water bowl level and increase the height difference by 1 inch. A steeper slope makes it harder to pump water and lowers the water flow rate.

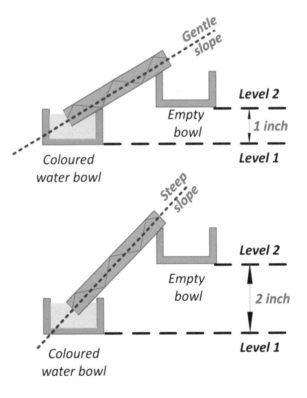

Rotation

The speed at which you rotate the screw pump determines the quantity of water being pumped and the time it takes to pump that quantity. The number of revolutions you make within a defined period is known as the rotational speed, and it is measured in revolutions per minute (rpm). A higher rotational speed results in a higher water flow rate from your screw pump. However, you could reach the maximum flow rate no matter how fast you rotate the pump due to the tubing size.

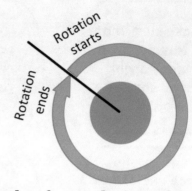

Example of 1 revolution where the rotation ends at the same starting point. The number of revolutions per minute (rpm) describes the rotational speed. You can calculate your rotational speed by counting the number of complete turns (revolutions) in 1 minute when you rotate your screw pump

Troubleshooting

	Fault	Solution
1	The screw pump is not picking up any water when you turn the bottle	⚙ Adjust the pump such that the opening of the tubing is underwater ⚙ Turn the pump in the direction that scoops water; only one direction works out
2	The screw pump is not picking up enough water	⚙ Adjust the height between the coloured water bowl and the empty bowl. The empty bowl should be raised 1-2 inches above the level of the coloured water bowl ⚙ Try to adjust the period between the wrapped tubing. Ideally, it would be best if you aimed for equal periods. Divide the length of the water bottle by the number of times you wrapped the tubing around the bottle to calculate your period

How it works

⊚ **Positive Displacement**: The Egyptian screw pump moves fluid upward, utilizing a screw mechanism inside a hollow tube.

⚒ **Mechanical Power**: The screw is turned by various power sources: human effort, windmills, animals, or motors.

💧 **Scooping Action**: Each turn of the screw captures water in the first round of the tubing, or 'pocket.'

⬅ **Sequential Lifting**: Subsequent turns transfer water from one pocket to the next higher one while simultaneously gathering more water at the base.

📈 **Continuous Movement**: With each rotation, the water ascends through the pockets until it pours out from the top of the tubing.

Explore

💧 **Measure the Output**: Determine how much water your screw pump transferred into the higher bowl. To find the flow rate, divide the volume of water by the time it took to pump.

🕐 **Count the Turns**: Keep track of how many rotations you made to fill the elevated bowl. Calculate your rotational speed by dividing the total number of turns by the time they took.

📏 **Experiment with Tubing Size**: Switch to ½-inch diameter tubing and note the time to fill the upper bowl. Compare this with the results using ¼-inch tubing to analyze the differences in flow rate.

🌡 **Test Temperature Effects**: Use water at different temperatures and observe any changes in the pumping efficiency or flow rate.

💪 **Vary the Power Source**: Try turning the screw with different methods, such as by hand, using a small motor, or attaching a handle to simulate windmill action, and note any changes in the water transfer rate.

Fun Facts: Ancient Egyptian Technologies

Ancient Egyptians formed the first civilization in the world. Their civilization was one of the most powerful and influential for 3000 years (3100 B.C. – 30 B.C.). Their inventions and technological advancements played a significant role in developing later civilizations. These advancements included building large constructions, such as the pyramids, and creating simple machines like levers and screw pumps.

One of the most important inventions of ancient Egyptians was writing, which allowed them to keep accurate records and control their large empire. They wrote on sheets from the "papyrus" plant to maintain important documents. The word "paper" came from the Egyptian "papyrus" sheets.

Hieroglyph was a phonetic writing system based on how humans make and perceive sounds. This system served as the basis for Hebrew, Greek, and Latin alphabets.

Architectural Marvels: The Great Pyramid of Giza, built around 2580–2560 BC, is a testament to ancient Egyptian engineering. It was the tallest man-made structure for over 3,800 years and was constructed with such precision that modern engineers still debate how it was achieved without the wheel or iron tools.

Ancient Egyptians studied a variety of medicines and cures. The Edwin Smith Papyrus was the earliest medical book containing recipes that addressed different ailments. This book is considered the first document that started neuroscience.

The Egyptians used more than 160 plant products and animal feces in preparing their medicines.

Egyptians developed a good understanding of mathematics and geometry, which helped them build the pyramids, castles, and other large structures. Their structures were among the largest constructions ever built by humans. They used tools, including limestones, wooden mallets, and stone hammers, to create these large structures and religious sculptures.

Egyptians used numbers, including a decimal system, to track business transactions. Their numbers were presented using factors of 10, such as 1, 10, 100, etc. For example, to write the number 42, they would write down 4 number 10 and 2 number 1.

(4) Turbo Glider

Get ready to soar with the 'Turbo Glider' experiment! Unlike your everyday paper airplane, this glider taps into the exciting world of aerodynamics using basic materials and the interplay of forces such as thrust, drag, lift, and gravity. This experiment allows you to explore various designs and understand how these forces work together to keep your glider smoothly sailing through the air. Discover the joy of crafting a glider that flies and glides beautifully in a well-balanced trajectory.

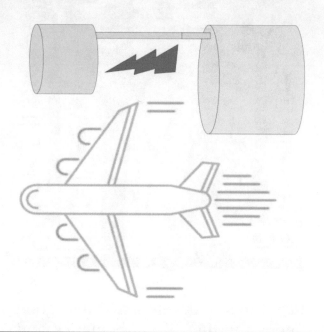

Concepts: Forces, motion, lift, drag, weight

Material

⚙ Paper – pick your favourite colour

⚙ A straw

⚙ Tape or glue

⚙ Scissors

⚙ Paper clips

Instructions

(1) Measure 1" to 2" from the longer edge of your paper, mark with a ruler and cut. The length should be between 11" and 15". This will be used for the bigger hoop

(2) Measure 1" to 2" from the shorter edge of your paper, mark with a ruler and cut. The length should be between 7" and 10". This will be used for the smaller hoop

(3) Turn each strip into a ring by taping or gluing the ends together with a 1/2" overlap. You should have one big hoop and one smaller hoop

(4) Attach your straw to the hoops. Tape of glue one end of the straw to the inside of the big hoop and the other end to the inside of the smaller hoop

(5) You may attach your straw to the hoops using paper clips instead of tape or glue. Both methods work fine

(6) Find a space with enough room to launch your turbo glider. Throw the glider with the small hoop facing forward and watch if flying fast in a straight line

How it works

➡ **Thrust Force**: Throwing the glider initiates a forward push, propelling it in the direction of motion.

⬆ **Lift Force**: Simultaneously, an upward force lifts the glider, countering gravity.

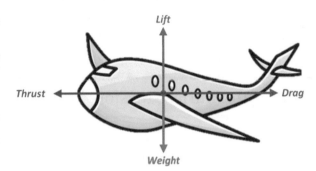

⭕ **Drag Force**: The large hoop encounters air resistance, creating a force opposite to thrust, helping to stabilize the glider.

⚖ **Balance of Forces**: Thrust and drag work together to keep the straw and glider level during flight.

⬇ **Gravity's Pull**: The weight of the glider, influenced by gravity, pulls it downwards, opposing the lift.

🌐 **Landing Mechanism**: As the lift diminishes, gravity eventually brings the glider back down to Earth.

Explore

📏 **Vary the Straw Lengths**: Conduct the experiment with straws of different lengths. Observe which glider travels faster and which one remains airborne longer.

⚫ **Experiment with Hoop Sizes**: Change the sizes of the hoops and test each glider. Notice how the hoop size influences the duration the glider stays aloft.

(5) Soap-Fueled Boat

Set sail on a soapy adventure with the 'Soap-Fueled Boat' experiment! Have you ever imagined a boat gliding through water, powered by nothing but soap? It's possible, thanks to the fascinating properties of soap in reducing water's surface tension. This experiment lets you construct your very own boat using everyday materials. Once your craft is ready, add a drop of liquid soap and watch in amazement as it zips across the water's surface!

Concepts: Surface tension, Forces, Marangoni effect

Material

* A foam tray (like the one they sell meat in) or a cardboard
* Scissors and glue
* A bowl filled with water
* Liquid soap
* A toothpick

Instructions

(1) Draw a boat shaped arrow on foam tray or cardboard and use the scissors to cut it, as shown in the illustration

(2) Cut a U-shaped notch at approximately 1/3 the foam tray, as shown in the illustration

(3) Place the boat in a bowl filled with water, on in a plugged sink filled with water

(4) Pour a few drops of liquid soap on the toothpick. Use the toothpick to coat the inside of the notch with liquid soap

(5) Fueled by the liquid soap, your boat will start to move forward across the water

(6) If the boat stopped moving, refuel it again with more liquid soap and watch what happens

Illustrations

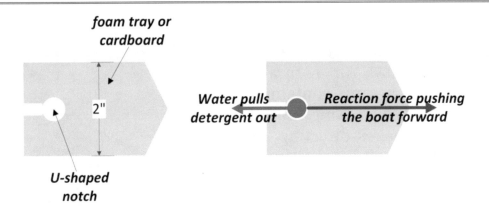

foam tray or cardboard

2"

U-shaped notch

Water pulls detergent out

Reaction force pushing the boat forward

How it works

💧 **Surface Tension Flow**: Fluids move from lower to higher surface tension areas, a phenomenon known as the Marangoni effect.

🔍 **Defining Surface Tension**: Surface tension is the measure of how fluid molecules stick together. Water's surface tension is higher than that of soap.

🚣 **Soap Propulsion**: Adding a drop of soap decreases the water's surface tension behind the boat. The higher-tension water ahead pulls the boat forward, creating thrust.

🧼 **Spreading Soap Molecules**: Soap molecules spread across the water, gradually equalizing the water's surface tension with the soap's.

⚠️ **Limit of Movement**: Once the water and soap surface tensions equalize, additional soap drops no longer move the boat, as there's no tension gradient to create thrust.

Explore

Experiment with Different Soap Types: Try the experiment using various types of liquid soap, such as dish soap, hand soap, or even shampoo. Observe how the different chemical compositions of these soaps affect the boat's speed and movement. Do some soaps propel the boat faster or further than others?

(6) High-Pressure Air Cannon

Get ready to launch into the world of physics with the 'High-Pressure Air Cannon' experiment! Air naturally expands to occupy any container, with its molecules moving in all directions. This makes directing air in a specific path quite a challenge. However, this experiment turns that challenge into fun! Using just a few simple materials, you'll construct an air cannon that harnesses the power of air molecules and channels them into high-pressure air. Prepare to be amazed by the force you can generate with nothing more than air!

Concepts: Airflow, air molecules, torus

Material

 A plastic or paper cup
 A balloon

 Scissors
 Duct tape

Instructions

(1) Use your scissors to cut a hole in the bottom of the plastic cup. The hole should be in the centre and smaller than the bottom

(2) Blow up the balloon to stretch it out and deflate it. Use the scissors to cut off the neck of the balloon

(3) Stretch the balloon over the lip of the cup to cover the top opening completely. Leave some excess balloon on the sides of the lip

(4) Use duct tape to secure the balloon on the cup lip. They should be as air-tight as possible

(5) Hold your air cannon with the hole facing away from you. Pinch and pull the centre of stretched balloon and then release to fire

(6) Aim at lightweight objects, such as a piece of toilet paper, a piece of popcorn, or a cotton ball, and record how far it moves when you fire

Illustrations

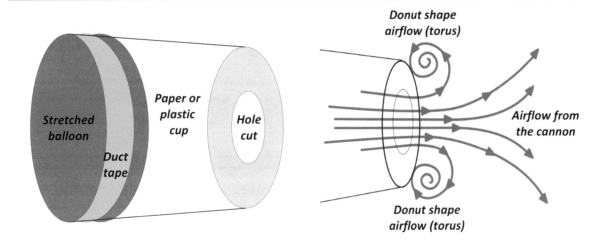

Stretched balloon

Duct tape

Paper or plastic cup

Hole cut

Donut shape airflow (torus)

Airflow from the cannon

Donut shape airflow (torus)

How it works

🌀 **Vortex Creation**: The vortex cannon exerts force on the air molecules trapped inside the cup.

🎈 **Balloon Release Impact**: Releasing the stretched balloon propels it into the air inside, driving the molecules towards the hole.

🌀 **Doughnut-Shaped Airflow**: The air shot from the cannon forms a spinning ring or torus, a vortex that travels outward.

⚙ **Torus Dynamics**: This torus shape occurs because air in the middle speeds ahead, while friction along the edges slows down the airflow, causing it to curl back.

(7) Nail Magnet

Embark on a journey through the captivating world of electromagnetism, where electricity and magnetism converge to perform incredible feats. In this field, a simple electric current passing through a wire can magically transform it into a magnet, with the power to attract ferromagnetic materials like iron and steel. Get ready to be an engineer and construct your very own potent magnet. By coiling an electric wire around a ferromagnetic core—such as an iron nail—you'll witness the creation of an electromagnet right before your eyes in this electrifying experiment!

Concepts: Electricity, magnetism, electromagnetism, magnetic field

Material

- ❖ *3-5 feet of thin insulated copper wire*
- ❖ *6-volt battery*
- ❖ *Electric tape*
- ❖ *About 3-inch iron nail*
- ❖ *Paperclips*

Instructions

(1) Wrap the insulated copper wire around the nail. Leave around 8-inch of wire loose from both sides.

→

(2) Strip both ends of the wire by removing about 1-inch of the plastic coating

→

(3) Attach one stripped end of the wire to one side of the battery and the other end to the other side of the battery

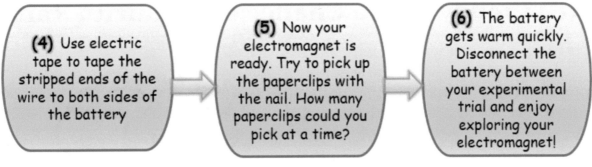

(4) Use electric tape to tape the stripped ends of the wire to both sides of the battery

(5) Now your electromagnet is ready. Try to pick up the paperclips with the nail. How many paperclips could you pick at a time?

(6) The battery gets warm quickly. Disconnect the battery between your experimental trial and enjoy exploring your electromagnet!

Illustrations

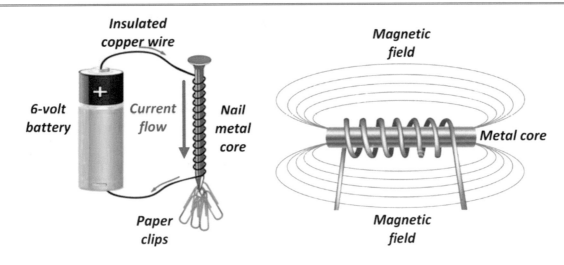

Insulated copper wire

6-volt battery

Current flow

Nail metal core

Paper clips

Magnetic field

Metal core

Magnetic field

How it works

Creating Electromagnets: Wrap a wire around a metal core to form an electromagnet.

Electric Current Activation: Connect the wire ends to a power source, such as a battery, to generate an electric current.

Magnetic Field Generation: The current flowing through the wire induces a magnetic field around the metal core

Controlled Power: Turn your electromagnet on and off by connecting or disconnecting it from the battery.

Permanent vs Electromagnet: Unlike always-on permanent magnets (like those on refrigerators), your electromagnet can be activated or deactivated as needed.

(8) Cloudy with a Chance of Colourful Rain

Have you ever wondered why rain pours down from some clouds but not others? The answer lies in the water cycle's continual dance of evaporation, condensation, and precipitation. With this experiment, you'll craft your own cloud and witness vibrant raindrops falling from it, offering a glimpse into the fascinating process of rain formation and the broader water cycle. Get ready to mix, pour, and watch your homemade cloud come alive with colorful precipitation!"

Concepts: water vapour, condensation, evaporation, precipitation

Material

- A water glass
- Shaving cream foam
- Food colouring
- Tap water

Instructions

(1) Fill the glass with water, leave 1/4th of the water glass empty $\rightarrow$ **(2)** Add a layer of shaving cream foam on top of the water in the glass $\rightarrow$ **(3)** Add several drops of food colouring. You may use different colours of your choice. Notice what happens to the food colouring drops

How it works

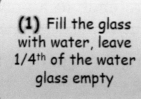 Adding Color Drops: Introduce food coloring to the shaving foam, and watch it trickle down, similar to rain falling from clouds.

◯ **Cloud Formation**: Clouds consist of water vapor, the gaseous state of water.

🌡 **Condensation Process**: A drop in air temperature causes water vapor to condense into liquid water droplets within the cloud.

🌧 **Raindrop Creation**: As these droplets multiply, they gather into larger drops.

⚖ **Cloud Weight**: When clouds become saturated with water droplets, they get too heavy.

⬣ **Gravity's Pull**: Excessive weight forces the drops to fall from the clouds to the Earth, driven by gravity.

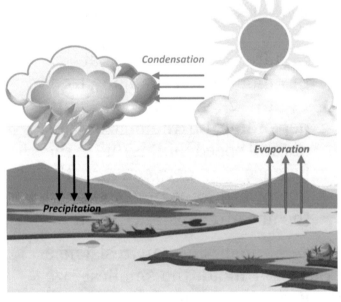

The water cycle is the process of water evaporating from the Earth, condensing in clouds, and falling on Earth again. The process consists of 3 steps:

(1) Water **evaporates** from the Earth's surface by turning from a liquid into a gas (water vapour)

(2) Water vapour rises due to heat from the sun and once it is high enough it **condenses** from water vapour into water droplets

(3) When the water droplets get heavy enough, they fall back (**precipitate)** to Earth as rain

Explore

💧 ❄ Temperature Variations: Test with water at varying temperatures. Observe how hot versus cold water affects the 'rainfall.'

◯ Foam Layer Thickness: Experiment with varying thicknesses of shaving foam. Note the difference between thin and thick 'cloud' layers on the rain simulation.

Fun Facts: Raindrops

The **size** of water droplets determines the **velocity** of a raindrop. **Gravity** pulls it down toward the Earth when a droplet becomes heavy enough. While falling, **air resistance** slows it down. Eventually, gravity and air resistance forces become equal and cancel each other, and the raindrop maintains a constant velocity, known as **terminal velocity**.

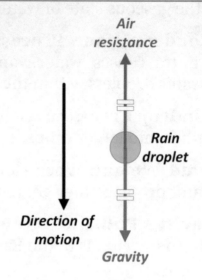

As raindrops grow larger, they reach a greater **terminal velocity**, which is the fastest speed they can fall. Typically, raindrops descend at a terminal velocity ranging from 15 to 25 miles per hour, depending on their size. This natural speed limit is due to the balance between the downward force of gravity and the upward resistance of air

Raindrops do not get much larger than ¼ inch since air resistance break them up when they fall. On the other hand, the smallest size possible for raindrops is 1/25th inch since they don't fall very well below this size. This small size is known as **drizzle-size raindrops**, which fall at a low terminal velocity of around 4 miles per hour.

For an average size raindrop falling from a height of 2500 ft at a terminal velocity of 14 miles per hour, it will take around 2 minutes to reach the ground! For a larger raindrop falling from the same height at a terminal velocity of 20 miles per hour, it will take around 7 minutes to reach the ground!

(9) Candle Carousel

Discover the magic of energy transformation with the 'Candle Carousel' experiment! Unlike traditional carousels powered by electricity, this unique carousel harnesses thermal energy from candles and converts it into mechanical energy. The secret lies in the rising hot air from lit candles, which gently pushes the blades of a paper carousel, setting it into a graceful spin. Dive into this fascinating exploration of energy conversion and watch your carousel come to life!

Concepts: aerodynamics, heat, force, blade, fan

Material

- A straw
- A metal nut that fits the size of the straw, ¼ inch inner diameter works fine for most straws
- A handful of playdough
- Glue
- A paper plate

- 4 tealight candles
- A wooden skewer with sharp ends

- Scissors
- A flat tray
- A lighter

Instructions

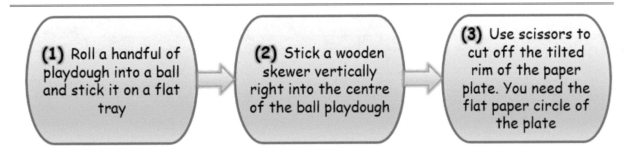

(1) Roll a handful of playdough into a ball and stick it on a flat tray

(2) Stick a wooden skewer vertically right into the centre of the ball playdough

(3) Use scissors to cut off the tilted rim of the paper plate. You need the flat paper circle of the plate

(4) Cut diagonal slits in the paper circle to create your carousel blades, as shown in the illustration. Do not cut all the way to the centre of the paper circle

(5) Use glue to attach the metal nut to the carousel right in the centre, as shown in the illustration

(6) Bend the edges of the blades downwards towards the metal nut at around 30 degrees from the carousel horizontal surface

(7) Insert one end of the straw in the metal nut. Make sure that the straw fits snugly in the nut.

(8) Make sure that the straw is perpendicular to the carousel. Once you get the straw as vertical as possible, apply glue to hold the straw in the metal nut

(9) Leave your setup for sometime until the glue dries. Once it dries, use scissors to cut the straw to a length of 3 inches.

(10) slide the wooden skewer in the straw from one side and insert the other side in the play dough

(11) Place the 4 candles on the tray under your carousel at equal intervals. Start lighting the candles one by one

(12) Observe the blade movement as you light more candles, does your carousel spin faster?

Illustrations

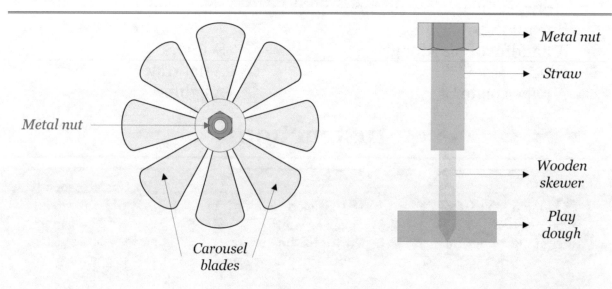

Metal nut

Carousel blades

Metal nut

Straw

Wooden skewer

Play dough

How it works

💧 **Candle Heat**: Candles generate heat that warms the air around them.

👆 **Rising Hot Air**: This heated air rises, moving above the cooler air.

⬅ **Blade Movement**: The rising warm air pushes against the carousel's tilted blades, causing them to spin around the straw shaft.

🌿 **Continuous Rotation**: As each blade turns, it makes way for the next to catch the upward moving air, creating a continuous motion.

⚙ **Importance of Tilt**: The specific tilt of the blades is crucial; without it, the carousel wouldn't spin.

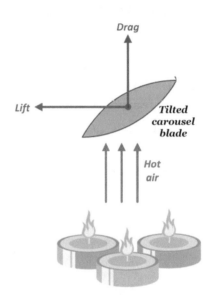

👊 **Lift and Drag Forces**: The hot air creates a drag force pushing up and a lift force that moves the blades horizontally, driving the carousel's spin.

⬅ **Sequential Blade Interaction**: After completing a rotation, each blade is once again propelled by the warm air, maintaining the carousel's momentum.

Explore

💨 **Airflow Observation**: Place a fan at varying distances from the carousel and note any differences in spin speed due to the additional airflow.

🎨 **Blade Design Testing**: Try blades of different shapes or sizes to see how they affect the carousel's spinning efficiency.

🕐 **Duration Test**: Measure how long the carousel spins with a set number of candles and compare the duration as you vary the candle count.

🌡 **Temperature Measurement**: Use a thermometer to measure the temperature above the candles and correlate it with the carousel's spin speed.

Fun Facts: Windmills

◎ **Wind Power to Energy**: Windmills transform wind power into rotational energy, with the first model appearing in Persia in the 9th century.

🏭 **Historical Uses**: Originally, windmills with 6 to 12 blades were utilized to grind grain and pump water.

🌐 **Global Spread**: After their inception in Persia, windmill technology spread across the world, with each region adapting the design to local conditions

💡 **Electricity Generation**: Wind turbines, evolving from windmills, harness wind to produce electricity, with the first one built in Scotland in the 19th century.

🌿 **Renewable Resource**: Today, wind turbines are a vital source of renewable energy, helping countries lessen fossil fuel dependence and reduce carbon emissions.

✈ **Modern Design**: Contemporary wind turbines typically have 3 large blades on a horizontal axis and are painted white for aircraft visibility.

⚙ Gearbox Function: A gearbox is used to accelerate the slow-moving blades to a speed that efficiently drives an electric generator.

📏 **Size Variations**: Turbine heights can vary from 66 to 262 feet to capture wind effectively.

📈 **Height Advantages**: The taller the wind turbine, the greater the wind speed it can exploit, as wind speed increases with altitude.

🏔 **Location Matters**: Windmills were historically placed on hills and open plains, where wind is abundant, mirroring the placement of modern wind turbines.

🔙 **Rotation Regulation**: Modern turbines can adjust blade rotation speed and direction according to the wind to maximize efficiency and protect the structure.

🔧 **Self-Maintenance**: Some advanced wind turbines have built-in sensors and systems that allow for remote monitoring and automatic adjustments for optimal performance.

🐦 **Wildlife Protection**: New turbine designs and placements are being explored to minimize the impact on birds and bats.

🤝 **Community Wind Projects**: Small-scale wind projects allow communities to generate their own power, fostering local energy independence.

🎚 **Acoustic Innovations**: Modern wind turbines have blades engineered to minimize noise, a result of advancements in aerodynamic design and materials.

⚙ **Smart Turbines**: Advances in technology have led to "smart" wind turbines equipped with sensors and computers that can predict weather changes, optimize energy production, and even perform self-diagnostics for maintenance.

(10) Rainbow Petal Project

Step into the world of botanical art with the Ranbow Petal Project!' Have you imagined turning a white flower into a canvas and painting it with the hues of your choice? This fascinating activity will show you how! Using the natural process known as transpiration, you'll draw colored water up through the stem of a flower, tinting its petals in vibrant shades. Prepare to be amazed as you witness the petals of a white carnation slowly soak up the rainbow from their watery palette and bloom into brilliant color before your eyes!

Concepts: transpiration, capillary action, adhesion, cohesion

Material

 White carnation flowers
 Food colouring in a variety of colours

 Small cups
 Tap water

Instructions

(1) Fill your cups with water. You may use as many cups as you like depending on how many colours you want to use

(2) Add 10-15 drops of food colouring into each cup, one colour each, and stir the mixture.

(3) Trim down at least 1/2 inch of stem off the flowers. Put each flower in one of the cups

(4) Keep the flowers in a cool place and check every couple of hours to observe any changes

(5) Depending on the type of flower, some flowers take longer to change colours. Keep the experiment running for 2-3 days

(6) If you wish to keep your flowers fresh for a long time, change the water entirely every 3 days

How it works

🌱 **Water Uptake**: Plants and flowers absorb water through their roots, or directly through the stems if cut from their roots.

🍀 **Capillary Action**: Water defies gravity and travels up the stem to the leaves and petals through a process called capillary action.

💧 **Evaporation and Suction**: As water evaporates from the plant's parts, it creates a suction force that pulls more water into the plant.

🚪 **Transpiration Process**: This entire journey of water, from absorption to evaporation, is known as transpiration.

The following factors participate in the water transportation process:

(1) **Capillary action**: tube-like tissues in the stem known as **xylem** bring water to different parts of the plant.

(2) **Adhesion**: adhesion forces allow water molecules to stick to xylem walls.

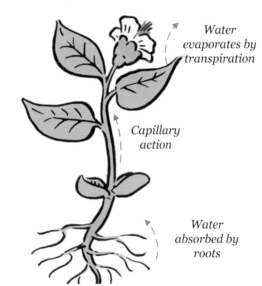

(3) *Cohesion:* cohesion forces attract water molecules to each other

(4) *Transpiration:* water evaporates from leaves and flowers, creating negative pressure in the xylem, which allows the plant to draw more water

Explore

📷 Color Mixing Experiment: Try mixing different food coloring in a single cup of water. Observe how the mixed colors travel up the flower and change its petal hues uniquely.

📊 Time-Lapse Observation: Record a time-lapse video of the color-changing process in the flower. Compare the rate of color change in different flowers or with varying amounts of food coloring.

(11) Bean in a Bag

Dive into the world of plant growth without the need for soil or traditional planting methods. In this activity, you'll be planting bean seeds inside a plastic bag, creating your own miniature indoor greenhouse. This unique setup allows you to closely observe the sprouting process right before your eyes. All you need is a sunny spot indoors, like a window, to witness the magic of nature as your beans begin their journey from seeds to sprouts. Get ready to watch the wonder of plant growth in the simplest, yet most revealing way!

Concepts: germination, photosynthesis

Material

- Bean seeds
- A Ziplock bag
- Paper towels
- Tape

Instructions

(1) Soak your bean seeds in water for 12 hours to get them ready to germinate and drain off the water when ready

(2) Take 2 pieces of paper towel, fold them together in half twice, and place them in the plastic bag

(3) Pour some water in the bag until the paper towel is wet. Place the 4 bean seeds on the top of the paper towel

(4) Take 1 piece of paper towel, fold it in half twice, and place it on top of your bean seeds. Add some water to wet the paper towel

(5) Seal the bag tightly and use tape to hang it on a sunny window. It takes 3 to 5 days for the seeds to germinate

(6) Keep the paper towel moist by spraying water inside the bag if you feel it dry. Do not oversaturate the paper towel with more water than needed

How it works

🌱 **Germination Process**: Seeds transform into plants via germination, which needs sufficient sunlight, the right temperature, water, and air.

⚙ **Photosynthesis Basics**: Plants produce their own food using water and carbon dioxide, combining these with sunlight energy.

🔄 **Water Transportation**: Water absorbed from the ground travels through the plant's stem to various parts.

🌿 **Energy Creation**: Nutrients in water, along with sunlight, fuel the process of photosynthesis, creating energy for the plant.

Photosynthesis is the process plants use to convert light energy into chemical energy. The chemical energy is stored in carbohydrates molecules, such as sugar, and synthesized from carbon dioxide and water. Oxygen gas escapes into the air through holes on the underside of the leaves.

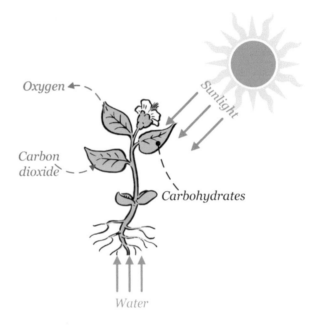

Carbon dioxide is a greenhouse gas that contributes to climate change and global warming. Plants absorb around 30% of all carbon dioxide emitted by humans. Photosynthesis is the main process responsible for maintaining the oxygen content of the Earth's atmosphere.

Explore

📝 **Growth Tracking**: Maintain a daily log to document the bean plant's growth - root length, stem changes, and leaf development.

⚙ 🌙 **Light Conditions Test**: Place beans in different light environments (direct sunlight, shade, artificial light) and note growth differences.

🌡 **Temperature Variation**: Experiment with beans in varied temperatures to observe the impact on germination and growth.

(12) Sunset in a Jar

Embark on a dazzling journey with the 'Sunset in a Jar' experiment and uncover the secrets of the sky's changing hues! Ever marveled at how the sky transitions from blue to a blend of red and orange during sunsets? This phenomenon is due to the white light from the sun, which is actually a mix of all the rainbow colors at different wavelengths. In this activity, you'll create your very own sunset inside a jar, observing the splendid color transformations as if you were watching the sun dip below the horizon. Get ready to capture the beauty of a sunset right in your home!

Concepts: Light, colour, wavelength

Material

 A tall glass jar

 Milk

 Water

 A flashlight

Instructions

(1) Fill the glass jar with tap water up to the top

(2) Shine the flashlight from the side of the jar and look from the front

(3) Observe the colour of water as you shine the flashlight. Can you see a light beam travelling through the water?

(4) Add one teaspoon of milk to the water and stir until they are well mixed

(5) Shine the flashlight from the side of the jar and look from the front. Observe changes in colours in the milk-water mixture as compared to water only jar

(6) Shine the flashlight from the top of the jar and look from the front. Check for any colour changes between the top and bottom of the jar

How it works

💡 **Flashlight as Sun**: The flashlight in the experiment represents the sun, and the milk particles mimic dust in the atmosphere.

🌙 **Clear Water Observation**: With only water in the jar, a narrow beam of light travels through, similar to sunlight at midday.

🥛 **Adding Milk**: Introducing milk to the jar creates cloudiness, as milk's fat particles, like atmospheric dust, scatter light.

⬤ **Blue Light Scattering**: When the flashlight shines from the side, blue light scatters in the water-milk mixture, resembling the slightly blue sky.

📱 **Longer Light Path**: Shining the flashlight from the top increases the light's travel distance, causing more scattering.

⬤ **Sunset Effect**: As light travels further in the jar, less blue light remains, turning the mixture orange, similar to the red-orange hues of a sunset.

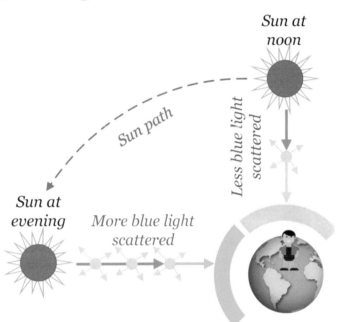

Explore

🔧 **Varying Milk Quantities**: Conduct the experiment multiple times, each time adding different amounts of milk to the jar. Observe how the color of the light changes with increased milk concentration.

😊 **Simulating Sun's Path**: Slowly rotate the flashlight from one side of the jar to the top (noon) and then down to the other side, mimicking the sun's movement from sunrise to sunset. Note the color shifts during this process.

🔨 **Different Light Sources**: Experiment with light sources of varying intensities and colors, like LED lights or colored flashlights, to see how they affect the color change in the jar.

Fun Facts: Sunlight

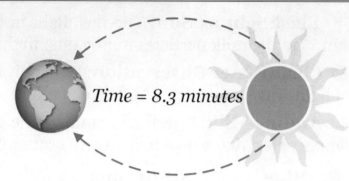

⬡ **Sun's Radiation**: The sun emits radiation that includes infrared, visible, and ultraviolet light.

🕐 **Travel Time to Earth**: It takes sunlight approximately 8.3 minutes to travel from the sun to Earth.

Time = 8.3 minutes

🌈 **True Nature of Sunlight**: Despite appearing in various hues during sunrise and sunset, sunlight is a mix of all colors, which looks white to our eyes.

🌧 **Rainbow Revelation**: A rainbow displays the different colors of sunlight, ranging from red to violet, each with its own wavelength.

●● **Wavelength Differences**: Violet and blue light have shorter wavelengths, while red light has the longest wavelength.

🖼 **Sunrise/Sunset Colors**: During sunrise and sunset, sunlight appears red or orange. This is because shorter wavelengths like blue and violet are scattered by the Earth's atmosphere.

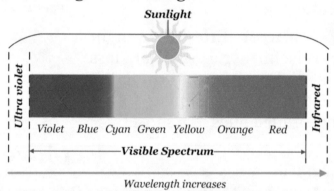

🖼 **Sunrise/Sunset Colors**: During sunrise and sunset, sunlight appears red or orange. This is because shorter wavelengths like blue and violet are scattered by the Earth's atmosphere.

🎨 **Long Wavelength Visibility**: Longer wavelengths such as red, yellow, and orange pass through the atmosphere and reach our eyes, giving sunrise and sunset their warm hues.

⬡ **Noon Sky Blue**: When the sun is high in the sky, such as at noon, blue light, which has a short wavelength, scatters upon hitting air molecules in the upper atmosphere, resulting in the sky's characteristic blue color.

(13) Energy in a Bottle

Have you ever wondered how energy can be harnessed and saved for later use? Capturing energy from natural sources and storing it is a key step towards reducing our dependence on traditional fuels like gas and electricity. In this engaging activity, you will construct your own energy storage system.

This hands-on experiment is a small-scale model of the advanced energy storage systems utilized in building technologies. Get ready to explore the fascinating concept of energy preservation right in your home!

Concepts: Energy storage systems, light properties, thermal mass

Material

- 2 equal size soda bottles
- 2 equal size balloons
- White spay paint
- Black spray paint

Instructions

(1) Use the spray paint to paint one of the bottles black and the other one white up to the neck of the bottles

(2) Leave the bottles for 1 hour until the paint dries

(3) Remove the bottle caps and stretch a balloon over the neck of the bottles. Make sure that the balloon fits tightly on the bottle neck

(4) Place the bottles outdoors in a shaded area for 1 hour and observe what happens to the balloons

(5) Place the bottles outdoors in direct sunlight for 1 hour and observe what happens to the balloons

(6) Return the bottles to the shaded area and leave them for 1 hour. Observe what happens to the balloons

How it works

Equal Air in Bottles: Both soda bottles contain the same amount of air, given their equal sizes.

Shaded Area Effect: In the shade, there's little to no change in the balloons, due to minimal energy transfer from the sun.

Sunlight Reaction: In direct sunlight, the balloon on the black bottle inflates as the air heats up and expands, while the balloon on the white bottle remains unchanged.

Color and Heat Absorption: Dark materials trap more heat as they absorb more light, whereas light materials reflect more light.

Light Absorption and Reflection: Perfect black bodies absorb all light, and perfect white bodies reflect all light, but real materials have varying degrees of light absorption, reflection, and transmission.

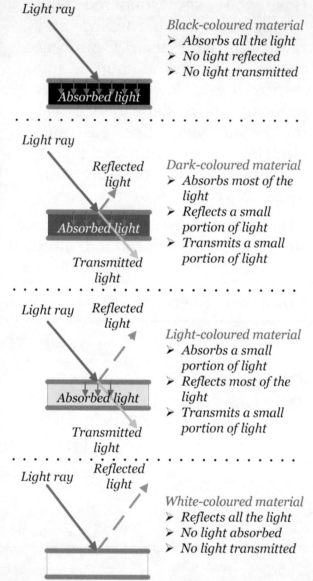

Material Selection in Engineering: Engineers select materials based on their specific properties of light absorption and reflection, which varies from perfect black or white.

Sunlight Heating: Both the black and white bottles warm up in sunlight, but the black bottle absorbs more heat.

Black Bottle's Heat Absorption: The increased heat in the black bottle causes air molecules inside it to rise faster and spread out more than in the white bottle.

☀ **Solar Heating Similarity**: The heating of the black bottle in sunlight resembles thermal mass usage in passive solar buildings.

🏠 **Thermal Mass Materials**: Thermal mass includes materials like concrete, brick, and water, which store energy.

😊 **Daytime Energy Absorption**: During the day, these materials absorb and store solar energy as thermal energy.

🌙 **Nighttime Energy Release**: After sunset, as indoor temperatures cool, the stored thermal energy is slowly released, heating the space.

💡 **Alternative to Conventional Heating**: This method reduces the need for additional heating sources like gas or electricity in winter.

Explore

🌈 **Color Variation Test**: Experiment with painting the bottles in different colors besides black and white. Observe how colors like red, blue, or green affect the balloon's inflation in sunlight.

🕐 **Time Interval Observations**: Change the duration the bottles are left in sunlight and shade. Note the differences in the balloon's inflation or deflation over shorter or longer periods.

🌡 **Temperature Monitoring**: Use a thermometer to measure the temperature inside each bottle. Compare how different bottle colors affect the internal temperature over time.

😎 **Sun Angle Experiment**: Adjust the angle of the bottles towards the sun. Try early morning, midday, and late afternoon positions to see how the sun's angle impacts the heating efficiency of each bottle.

🏠 **Indoor vs. Outdoor Comparison**: Conduct the experiment both indoors (near a sunny window) and outdoors to compare the effect of direct versus indirect sunlight on the bottles' heating.

(14) Climate Change in a Jar

Are you curious about the factors driving climate change and the steps we can take to safeguard our planet? The key lies in the balance of gases in our atmosphere, essential for sustaining life. When this balance shifts, it can have far-reaching impacts on all living beings. In this experiment, you'll create a model to understand the greenhouse effect and its role in climate change. By simulating this phenomenon in a jar, you'll gain insight into one of the most pressing environmental issues of our time and the importance of maintaining ecological harmony on Earth!

Concepts: Greenhouse effect, climate change

Material

- 3 glass jars
- White vinegar
- Elastic bands

- Baking soda
- Plastic wrap
- A thermometer (optional)

Instructions

(1) Label the first jar as "vinegar" and fill 1/3rd of the jar with vinegar. Cover the jar with a plastic wrap and secure it with an elastic band

(2) Label the second jar as "baking soda" and add 1 tablespoon of baking soda to the jar. Cover the jar with a plastic wrap and secure it with an elastic band

(3) Label the third jar as "reaction". This jar will be used to create a chemical reaction, you should prepare to seal the jar quickly!

(4) Fill 1/3rd of the "reaction" jar with vinegar and add 1 tablespoon of baking soda. Quickly Cover the jar with a plastic wrap and secure it with an elastic band

(5) Place the three jars in front of a heat source for 15 minutes. You could use natural sunlight from a window or a heat radiator. Make sure that the jars are heated evenly

(6) Make a small slit in the plastic wrap and insert a thermometer to take the temperature inside each jar. Record your results for the three jars

How it works

🌡️ **➕** 🔬 **Higher Temperature from Reaction**: You must have noticed that the temperature of the chemical reaction jar is higher than the temperatures of the vinegar-only and baking soda-only jars. Vinegar is an acid, whereas baking soda is a base; when mixed, a chemical reaction takes place as follows:

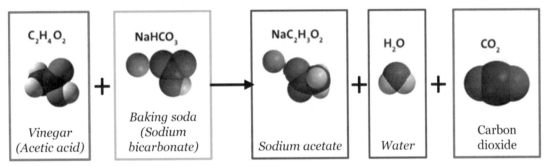

$C_2H_4O_2$ — Vinegar (Acetic acid) + $NaHCO_3$ — Baking soda (Sodium bicarbonate) → $NaC_2H_3O_2$ — Sodium acetate + H_2O — Water + CO_2 — Carbon dioxide

✏️ **Chemical Reaction & CO2**: The vinegar and baking soda mix in the experiment produces CO2 gas, a key greenhouse gas.

🌡️ **Temperature Rise in Jar**: The 'reaction' jar traps more heat due to the presence of CO2, leading to a higher temperature compared to the other jars when heated.

🌢 **Fossil Fuels & CO2 Emissions**: Burning fossil fuels for transportation, heating, cooling, and industrial processes releases CO2 into the atmosphere.

🌍 **Heat Trapping Effect**: CO2 in the atmosphere traps heat, causing Earth's global average temperature to increase.

🚨 **Climate Threat**: This rise in temperature poses a threat to all forms of life by altering climates and ecosystems.

(15) Secrets of Acid Rain

Discover the hidden dangers of rain with "Secrets of Acid Rain." This experiment unveils the hidden side of precipitation—when rain turns acidic, it can damage everything from delicate plants to sturdy buildings. Explore the science of acid rain through a simple and safe experiment that brings this environmental issue to life, right in your jar! Get ready to dazzle your friends and family with your eco-knowledge and help save the planet from the danger of acid rain!

Concepts: Acid rain, pollution, pH value

Material

- 2 glass jars
- White vinegar
- 2 small glasses
- Elastic bands
- 6 marbles
- Plastic wrap
- 2 similar flowers

Instructions

(1) Fill the two small glasses with water and place one flower in each glass. You may trim the flower stem to make sure it fits inside the glass

(2) Place each glass with a flower in one of the jars. Make sure there is a space of 1-2 inches between the top of the flower and the jar neck

(3) Label the first jar as "water" and pour 1/2 cup of water in the jar. Make sure that this water does not touch the flower or the glass. It should be in the bottom of the jar

(4) Label the second jar as "vinegar" and pour 1/2 cup of vinegar in the jar. Make sure that the vinegar does not touch the flower or the glass. It should be in the bottom of the jar

(5) Cover each jar with a plastic wrap and secure it with an elastic band. Place 3 marbles on top of the plastic wrap on each jar

(6) Place the two jars outdoor under direct sunlight. leave the jars outdoors until next day and record your observations regarding the flowers

How it works

🌱 **Vinegar as Acid Rain**: In this experiment, you used vinegar, an acid with a pH value of around 3, to mimic the effect of acid rain on the flowers.

⚙ **Sunlight Evaporation**: When you place the two jars under direct sunlight, the water in the first jar and the water and vinegar in the second jar start to evaporate, changing their state from a liquid into gas.

💧 **Condensation Process**: As evaporated gas meets the cooler surfaces of the jar and plastic wrap, it turns back into liquid, mimicking rain.

⚖ **Marble Effect**: The marbles added weight to the centre of the plastic wrap, which caused the water droplets to fall directly on the flowers.

📊 **pH Scale**: Ranges from 0-14; 7 is neutral, below 7 is acidic, and above 7 is basic.

🔬 **Acidic Mixture**: Mixing water (pH 7) and vinegar (pH 3) created a mildly acidic solution, similar to acid rain's pH, which is often at or below 5.

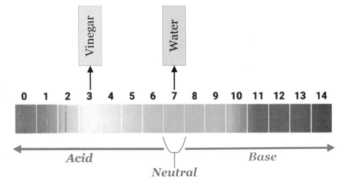

🌸 **Plant Health**: The flower in the acidic mixture showed signs of wilting, similar to the detrimental effects of acid rain on vegetation.

⛏ **Acid Rain Causes**: Emissions of sulfur dioxide (SO_2) and nitrogen oxides (NO_2) from burning fossil fuels react with water in the atmosphere to form sulfuric (H_2SO_4) and nitric (HNO_3) acids, resulting in acid rain.

Fun Facts: Climate Change

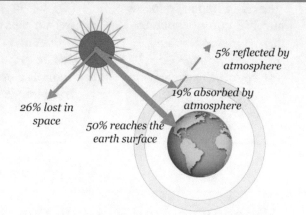

⬡ **Solar Radiation Reach**: Approximately 50% of the sun's radiation penetrates the atmosphere and reaches Earth's surface.

🛰 **Radiation Lost in Space**: About 26% of solar radiation is lost in space.

☁ **Atmospheric Absorption**: Around 19% of solar radiation is absorbed by the atmosphere and clouds.

🌍 **Heat Transformation**: The absorbed solar radiation is converted into heat, which plays a crucial role in maintaining Earth's temperature and warming surface waters.

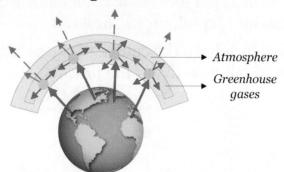

🌎 **Natural Process**: The greenhouse effect is a naturally occurring phenomenon.

🌡 **Heat Trapping**: It involves atmospheric gases trapping heat within the Earth's atmosphere.

⚖ **Energy Balance**: This process maintains a balance between energy entering and exiting Earth's atmosphere to maintain the Earth's temperature and make life possible on our planet.

🌡 **Heat Absorption**: Earth reflects some of the sun's heat back into space. Atmospheric greenhouse gases, like carbon dioxide, trap Earth's radiated heat, keeping Earth's climate warm enough for life.

🏭 **Human Impact**: Human activities, such as burning fossil fuels, increase greenhouse gas levels. High carbon dioxide from fossil fuels accumulates in the atmosphere. More greenhouse gases mean more trapped heat and a rise in Earth's temperature.

🌡 **Climate Change**: Excessive heat leads to significant climate and environmental changes.

(16) Create a Bouncy Ball

Get ready to become a young scientist in your own home lab! This exciting experiment will show you the secrets behind a bouncy ball's springy action. By mixing everyday household items, you'll stir up a fun chemical reaction that turns gooey glue into a super bouncy sphere. Discover how to tweak your formula for even more durable, high-flying bouncy balls. It's time to put on your thinking caps, blend your materials, and bounce into the world of science!

Concepts: Chemical reaction, polymers

Material

- ½ cup of warm water
- 2 small cups
- 2 tablespoons of glue
- Food colouring

- 1 plastic spoon
- 1 tablespoon of borax (used as a detergent in the laundry)
- 1 tablespoon of cornstarch

Instructions

(1) Use the first cup to mix 1 tablespoon of borax with 1/2 cup of warm water. Stir the mixture with a plastic spoon until the borax dissolves completely in the water

(2) Use the second cup to mix 1 tablespoon of cornstarch with 2 tablespoons of glue. Add 4-5 drops of your favourite food colouring to the mixture

(3) Add one spoon of borax mixture from the first cup into the second cup and stir to mix them together until it becomes hard to stir and the mixture turns into a rubbery texture

(4) Remove the mixture from the second cup with your hand. Place it between your two hands and roll the mixture into a ball

(5) If you feel the ball is still too slimy, dip it inside the borax mixture cup to harden it

(6) Continue rolling the balls with your hands until it is smooth and round. Try your bouncy ball and adjust by rolling more if needed

How it works

Chemical Reaction: Mixing borax with glue triggers a reaction that creates a polymer.

Polymer Formation: A polymer consists of repeated molecules linked together in a long chain.

Unique Properties: These polymers have high molecular mass, granting them toughness and elasticity.

Natural and Synthetic: Polymers can be natural (like wool, silk, and rubber) or synthetic (such as nylon and plastic).

Cornstarch Role: Adding cornstarch strengthens the bonds between large polymer molecules, helping the ball maintain its shape.

Explore

Borax and Glue Ratios: Experiment with varying amounts of borax and glue to discover the combination that yields the highest bounce.

Cornstarch Variation: Adjust the quantity of cornstarch and observe its impact on the ball's durability and bounciness.

Color Experiments: Try using different colors or combinations of food coloring to see if it affects the bounce or texture of the ball.

Curing Time Test: Experiment with different curing times before testing the ball's bounce, to see if longer or shorter setting periods make a difference.

(17) Cabbage Liquid Indicator

Have you imagined that a common vegetable like red cabbage could unveil the secret nature of household liquids? In this fascinating activity, you'll transform cabbage into a magical color-changing juice to explore the world of acids and bases. By testing various solutions from fruit juices to soda pops, you'll discover their hidden chemical properties and watch as your cabbage indicator reveals a rainbow of colors based on each solution's acidity or alkalinity. Get ready to turn your kitchen into a chemistry lab and see science come to life in vibrant hues!

Concepts: Acid, base, pH value

Material

- Red cabbage
- A boiling pot
- A strainer
- Paper cups

- A medicine dropper
- 2 large bowls
- Solutions you want to test, such as fruit juices, vinegar, soda pops, etc.

Instructions

(1) Shred a small red cabbage and place the pieces into a boiling pot. Add boiling water until the cabbage is fully covered with water

(2) Leave the cabbage in the boiling water for 30 minutes. Stir every 10 minutes to spread the cabbage in the water

(3) Place a strainer over a large bowl and pour the cabbage water mixture through the strainer. Press down the bulb in the strainer using a spoon to squeeze as much liquid as possible

(4) The liquid squeezed from the cabbage into the bowl should be purple or dark blue in colour. You will use this cabbage liquid indicator to test other solutions

(5) Select any solution you like, such as fruit juices, vinegar, or pop soda. Use a separate paper cup for each solution you want to test

(6) Fill half of the paper cup with your cabbage liquid indicator. Add drops of the liquid you want to test until you see changes in colour. Swirl the cup as you add the drops

How it works

pH Indicator Creation: You have successfully created a pH indicator using red cabbage liquid to test solution acidity or alkalinity.

Anthocyanin in Cabbage: Red cabbage contains anthocyanin, a pigment that changes color in different pH environments.

Color Changes: The purple cabbage liquid turns red with acidic solutions (pH < 7) and bluish-green with basic solutions (pH > 7).

pH Scale Understanding: pH value ranges from 0 to 14, with 7 being neutral like water. Below 7 indicates acidity, above 7 indicates alkalinity.

Color Chart Reference: The following chart indicates the pH value for the possible colour you could get from different solutions you test using your cabbage indicator:

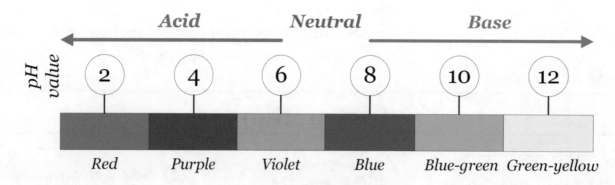

Explore

Acid-Base Mixing: Mix acidic and basic solutions in different proportions and observe how the cabbage indicator's color changes. This can help you understand the neutralization process between acids and bases.

(18) Glowing Bouncy Egg

In this exciting engineering journey, you'll use common household items to change an egg's structure into a glowing, bouncy marvel. By harnessing the unique chemical reactions between eggshells and vinegar, and adding a twist with a yellow highlighter, you'll create an egg that not only glows but also bounces! Prepare to be amazed as you witness the transformation of an everyday egg into a glowing orb of wonder.

Concepts: chemical reaction, semi-permeable, osmosis

Material

- 1 raw egg
- A yellow highlighter marker
- Vinegar
- A glass jar

Instructions

(1) Take the polyester cylinder of the highlighter marker out and squeeze its content in a glass jar. Take as much ink from the highlighter as possible

(2) Place a raw egg in the glass jar on the ink extracted from the highlighter

(3) Pour vinegar in the glass jar up to the top of the egg. You will see tiny bubbles starting to cover the egg

(4) Leave the egg in the vinegar-filled glass jar for 2 days until the shell dissolves leaving the membrane. Observe changes in the liquid colour

(5) Take the egg out of the jar. If the shell did not dissolve completely, rub the shell with your fingers to reveal the membrane

(6) Turn off the light and shine a flashlight on the egg and watch it glow. Bounce the egg softly on the table to check how it bounces

How it works

🥚 **Egg in Vinegar-Highlighter Mix**: Placing the egg in a solution of vinegar and highlighter ink causes it to expand.

🔬 **Semi-Permeable Membrane**: The egg's membrane is semi-permeable, meaning it allows certain molecules and ions to pass through.

💧 **Osmosis Process**: This membrane expansion happens through osmosis, where specific molecules move through the semi-permeable membrane.

💧 **Osmosis** is the process of moving molecules from a region of high-water potential to a region of low water potential in the direction that equalizes the concentration on the two sides.

🥚 **Equilibrium**: An egg has a lower concentration of water than vinegar. When you place the **egg** in **vinegar**, water molecules move from the vinegar (higher water potential) into the egg (lower water potential) through the semi-permeable membrane to reach equilibrium.

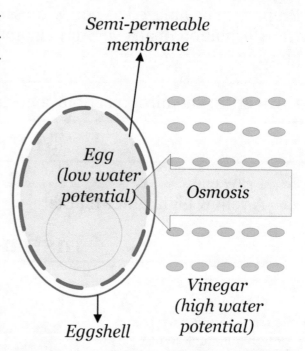

🕐 **Two-Day Process**: Leaving the egg in the vinegar-highlighter solution for two days results in the vinegar dissolving the eggshell.

🖊️ **Ink Absorption and Glow**: The egg's membrane permits water and highlighter ink to penetrate via osmosis, causing the egg to expand, become bouncy, and glow from the ink inside.

Explore

🕐 **Time Variation**: Adjust the duration the egg is left in the vinegar-highlighter solution. Test shorter or longer periods to see how this affects the egg's bounciness and glow intensity.

(19) Milky Way to Plastic

Prepare to be amazed with the "Milky Way to Plastic" experiment! Ever wondered how a simple liquid like milk could transform into something as solid as plastic? In the early 1900s, milk was a popular ingredient for creating plastic products, and now it's your turn to try this incredible transformation. In this fun and educational experiment, you'll mix milk with vinegar to craft your very own star-shaped plastic. Get ready to explore the fascinating process of turning everyday milk into a solid, colorful plastic creation!

Concepts: chemical reaction, polymers, plastic, ecosystem

Material

- 1 cup of milk with high-fat content
- White vinegar
- A heatproof mug
- A large bowl
- Paper towels
- Food colouring
- A strainer
- A star-shaped cookie cutter

Instructions

(1) Pour 1 cup of fatty milk in a heat proof mug and heat it in the microwave until the milk is steaming. Do not overboil the milk

(2) Add 4 teaspoons of white vinegar to the milk and stir for a few minutes. The milk should start to form white curds as you stir

(3) When the milk has curdled, pour the mixture into a bowl using a strainer. Press down the curds in the strainer using a spoon to squeeze the liquid

(4) Place two paper towels in a separate bowl. Place the curds collected in the strainer on the paper towels

(5) Fold the paper towels over the curds and squeeze to remove any liquid remaining. If needed, use additional paper towels until the curds are dry

(6) Knead the curds together. Add your favourite food colouring. Press and fold until you create a uniform ball

(7) Spread the plastic dough and mold a star shape using a star-shaped cookie cutter. Remove the additional parts of the dough

(8) Leave the plastic star to dry for 48 hours. You may place it near a sunny window to dry it faster

(9) When the plastic star is dry and hard, Use a marker of your favourite colour to paint the star

How it works

Milk and Vinegar Reaction: Vinegar is an acid with a pH value of around 3; when you add vinegar to hot milk, the molecules of a protein found in milk, called casein, unfold and rearrange themselves into long chains, forming the solid curds in the mixture. These long chains are called polymers.

Polymerization Process: Similarly, the chemical reaction that produces plastic is called polymerization. This reaction produces long chains of repeated single molecular units called monomers. Monomers are mainly made from fossil fuel chemicals.

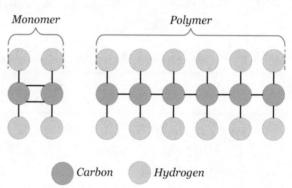

Monomer   Polymer

Carbon   Hydrogen

Natural Polymer Plastic: This experiment creates a natural polymer plastic using milk and vinegar, unlike conventional plastics made from petroleum.

Petroleum-Based Plastics: Regular plastics, sourced from petroleum, are non-biodegradable, leading to environmental accumulation and harm, especially in marine ecosystems.

Explore

Color Experiments: Experiment with adding different food coloring to the milk before adding vinegar. Observe how various colors affect the appearance and texture of your plastic creation.

Curing Time Variation: Test different curing times for your plastic. Leave some to set for a shorter period and others for longer, and compare their hardness and durability.

Fun Facts: Plastic

Origin of Single-Use Plastics: Made primarily from fossil fuel chemicals, designed for one-time use before disposal.

Non-Biodegradable Nature: Plastic waste doesn't biodegrade; it breaks down into tiny particles, releasing toxic substances.

Environmental Impact: These particles, known as microplastics, persist in the environment, contaminating food and water sources.

Microplastics in Human Body: Microplastics have been discovered in human organs like lungs, livers, and kidneys, posing health risks.

Ubiquity of Single-Use Plastics: Single-use plastics have become an integral part of our daily life. We use these products without knowing they end up polluting our environment. Examples of single-use plastics include:

Water bottles	Shampoo bottles	Microwave dishes
Plastic bags	Milk bottles	Bottle caps
Plastic straws	Freezer bags	Microwave dishes
Plastic plates	Food wrappers	Potato Chip bags
Plastic cups	Ice cream containers	Biscuit trays

🚫 **Global Bans**: Several countries implemented bans on single-use plastics. People around the world are more aware of the threat plastics impose and started to take induvial actions, such as:

- Choose food with no plastic wrapping
- Carry reusable bags for shopping
- Refill containers, such as reusable water bottles and coffee mugs
- Clean beaches and rivers

(20) Apple Oxidation Challenge

Ever sliced an apple and watched it magically change color? This isn't magic but science in action! When apple slices meet the air, they start to turn brown due to a natural reaction with oxygen. But here's the twist: you can play the role of a food scientist and put the brakes on this browning process. Using everyday items like lemon juice and vinegar, you'll experiment with different methods to keep your apple slices looking fresh and crisp longer. Let's see if you can outsmart apple oxidation!

Concepts: Oxidization, melanin, enzyme

Material

- 2 apples of the same type
- White vinegar
- A cutting board
- Lemon juice
- Airtight container
- 3 plates

Instructions

(1) Place the two apples on a cutting board and cut the apples in half. Cut each half in half again. You will have 8 slices of apple

(2) Prepare 3 plates and label them as: air, water, and lemon juice. Place 2 slices of apple in each plate. Place the remaining 2 slices in an air tight container

(3) Pour 2 teaspoons of water on the slices in the water plate, and 2 teaspoons of lemon juice on the slices in the lemon juice plate

(4) Make sure that the water and lemon juice completely cover the top of the apple slices

(5) Leave the apple slices for two hours. Check every 30 minutes to watch the progress

(6) After two hours check the apple slices in the 3 plates and in the air tight container and record which appl slices are least brown

How it works

🍎 **Polyphenol Oxidases in Apples**: Apples contain enzymes called polyphenol oxidases (PPO).

✂️ **Oxidation Upon Cutting**: Cutting an apple speeds up the reaction between apple polyphenols and oxygen, leading to oxidation.

💙 **Melanin Formation**: This oxidation reaction forms melanin, giving the apple a brown color, known as enzymatic browning.

🍃 **Common in Other Fruits**: Enzymatic browning also occurs in bananas, pears, and eggplants.

☕ **Browning in Beverages**: Black tea, coffee, and cocoa get thcir dark color from similar enzymatic browning processes.

🔋 **Air Exposure**: Apple slices exposed directly to air brown the fastest due to increased oxygen interaction.

💧 **Water Coating Effect**: Water forms a barrier, slowing down enzymatic browning by limiting oxygen contact.

🍋 **Citric Acid in Lemon Juice**: Lemon juice's citric acid acts as an antioxidant, strongly protecting apple slices from air and delaying browning.

💾 **Airtight Container**: Placing apple slices in an airtight container minimizes oxygen exposure, slowing the oxidation process.

Explore

🌡️ **Temperature Effects**: Test how different storage temperatures (refrigerator vs. room temperature) affect the rate of enzymatic browning in these fruits.

🍵 **Beverage Experiment**: Brew black tea, coffee, or cocoa for varying lengths of time to see how the intensity of color changes, and relate this to the enzymatic browning process.

(21) Perfect Crisp Potato

Ever pondered the secret behind that delightful crunch? This experiment isn't just tasty – it's a journey into the science of cooking! You'll explore the fascinating world of food texture, specifically how to keep potatoes crisp. By diving into the effects of saltwater versus plain water on potato slices, you'll uncover the key to making fries with the perfect crispness. So, grab a potato, and let's slice, soak, and discover the science behind your favorite crispy snack!

Concepts: Osmosis, semi-permeable

Material

- 1 potato
- 2 water glasses
- A cutting board
- Salt
- Tap water

Instructions

(1) Label two water glasses as "water only" and "water-salt". Fill in the two glasses with water

(2) Add 3 tablespoons of salt in the glass labeled "water-salt". Stir the mixture for 1 minute

(3) Use a cutting board to slice up your potato into French fries style pieces

(4) Observe the initial colour of the potato pieces and check their texture and flexibility

(5) Place half the potato pieces in the "water only" glass and the other half in the "water-salt" glass. Leave them overnight

(6) Remove the pieces from the glasses and observe what happened to their colour and texture. Which glass contains more crispy pieces for you to fry?

How it works

🔘 **Purpose of Saltwater Soak**: Saltwater is used to soak potatoes because it draws out moisture from them, crucial for achieving crispiness.

💧 **Natural Moisture in Potatoes**: Potatoes naturally contain moisture, which is key in the osmosis process.

🧂 **Osmosis with Saltwater**: Placing potatoes in saltwater triggers osmosis, where moisture moves towards higher salt concentrations.

▨ **Moisture Reduction**: The osmotic process in saltwater reduces the moisture content in potato slices, making them drier.

🧁 **Crispier Outcome**: Reduced moisture from the saltwater soak leads to crispier fries upon cooking.

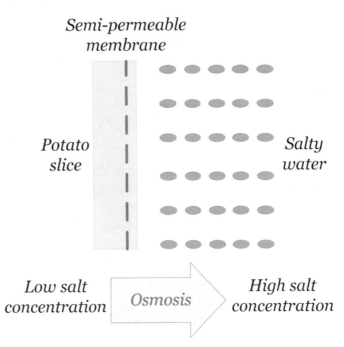

Explore

🔬 **Temperature Test**: Experiment with soaking potatoes in saltwater at different temperatures. Try cold, room temperature, and warm water to see how it affects crispiness.

🕐 **Soaking Duration**: Vary the soaking time in saltwater. Test short soaks versus longer soaks (e.g., 30 minutes vs. several hours) and observe the difference in crispiness.

🥔 **Different Potato Varieties**: Try the experiment with various types of potatoes. See how russet, red, sweet, or other potato varieties respond to the saltwater soak.

🔍 **Cooking Methods Comparison**: After soaking, cook the potatoes using different methods like baking, frying, or air frying. Compare which method produces the crispiest result.

(22) Magic Window Paper

Unlock the secrets of light with a sheet of paper in the 'Magic Window Paper' experiment. Discover how to manipulate an ordinary white paper to create a translucent effect, allowing you to peek through it as if by magic! Through this simple yet fascinating activity, you'll explore the principles of light absorption and transmission using everyday materials. Get ready to be amazed as you transform the paper into a see-through panel and learn about the science of light!

Concepts: Light properties, reflected light, transmitted light

Material

 1 sheet of white paper
 Oil (vegetable or olive)

 Tissue papers

Instructions

(1) Take a white sheet of paper and label one side as "front" and the other side as "back". in front of a light source, like a table lamp

(2) Hold the paper against a light source, like a table lamp. The "back" side should face the light as you look at the front side. Record your observations

(3) Turn around and look at the backside of the paper. You will look from the same side of the light. Record your observations

(4) Pour a few drops of oil on the centre of the paper. You may use a tissue to squeeze the drops of oil

(5) Hold the paper against the light. The "back" side facing the light while you look at the front side. Observe how the light is showing through the oil spot compared to the rest of the paper

(6) Turn around and look at the "front" side. Compare what you see from both sides to what you observed before you added the oil

How it works

◑ Light Reflection: The paper seems dark from the front when backlit; light bounces off the back and isn't seen from this angle.

☼ Direct Viewing: From the light's side, the paper's back shows up white; light reflects directly into your eyes, making it visible.

💧 **Oil Application**: Adding oil to the paper creates a translucent spot.

🌑 **Circle of Light**: This oiled area becomes visible as a bright circle when backlit.

✳ **Light Transmission**: Oil changes the paper's opacity, letting light through for your eyes to detect.

🔚 **When turned**: Observing from the light side shows a dark circle at the oil spot, contrasting with the surrounding white paper.

🗒 **Oil Effect**: The oil spot allows light to pass through, creating a visible dark circle.

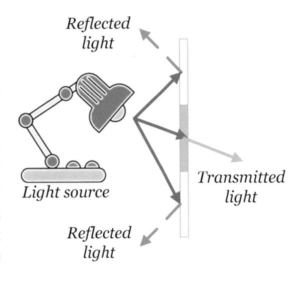

Reflected light

Transmitted light

Light source

Reflected light

☐ White paper side view
▨ Oil in the centre of paper

Explore

🔍 **Different Oils**: Try using various types of oils (vegetable, olive, coconut) to see if they affect the transparency of the paper differently.

🎨 **Colored Oils**: Mix food coloring with oil before applying to the paper to explore how colored oils interact with light and paper.

☺ **Natural Light Test**: Hold the paper with the oil spot against natural sunlight instead of artificial light to compare the effects on transparency.

🕯 **Varying Light Intensities**: Test the oil-treated paper against light sources of varying intensities, like a dim lamp versus a bright flashlight, to observe changes in transparency.

(23) Fireworks in a Jar

Imagine crafting your very own dazzling display of colors right in your kitchen! With "Liquid Fireworks: A Jar of Wonder," you'll combine everyday items to spark a vibrant dance of hues, mimicking real fireworks show. This experiment is a perfect blend of art and science, offering you a front-row seat to an underwater spectacle of colors as they burst and cascade in a jar. Grab your ingredients and get ready to be awed by the chemistry of colors!

Concepts: Chemical properties, density, molecular weight

Material

- A large glass jar
- 4 colours of food colouring
- A small bowl
- Vegetable oil
- Tap water
- A small tablespoon

Instructions

(1) Fill a large glass jar with warm water until it is 3/4th full

(2) Use a small bowl to add 4 tablespoons of vegetable oil. Choose 4 food colouring of your favourite and add 4 drops of each colour. Stir them together

(3) Pour the oil-food colouring mixture in the glass jar on top of the warm water. Watch your fireworks forming and record your observations

How it works

💧 **Water's Molecular Structure**: Water, being denser due to its molecular structure, is heavier than oil.

⚖️ **Density Difference**: In a mixture, water sinks below oil because of its greater density.

🌈 **Food Coloring Properties**: Food coloring is heavier than oil and only dissolves in water, not in oil.

🥄 **Mixing Oil and Color**: When the oil and food coloring mixture is added to water, the coloring drops sink through the oil layer.

✴️ **Fireworks Effect**: Upon reaching the water, these drops dissolve, creating a fireworks-like display in the jar.

💧🛢 **Immiscibility of Water and Oil**: Water and oil are immiscible, meaning they don't mix.

🔋 **Water's Polar Structure**: Water molecules are polar, with positive and negative charges at opposite ends.

🧲 **Molecular Attraction**: These charges cause water molecules to attract and stick to each other.

🔚 **Non-Polar Oil Molecules**: Oil molecules are non-polar, lacking these charges, and therefore don't adhere to other molecules.

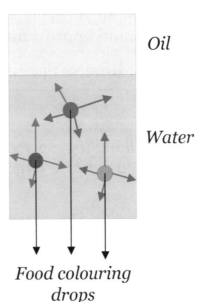

Oil

Water

Food colouring drops

Explore

🌡 **Temperature Variation**: Experiment with water at different temperatures (cold, room temperature, hot) to observe how it affects the behavior of oil and food coloring mixture.

🎨 **Color Mixing**: Try using different combinations of food coloring to see how the colors interact and create unique patterns in the oil and water mixture.

(24) Reverse Engineering

Did you know that engineers not only invent and build machines, tools, products, and structures but also take them apart? Reverse engineering allows engineers to determine technologies and components used in existing designs and investigate ways to improve them. You'll take apart a small toy to discover its inner workings in this activity. Learn how every piece fits together and what makes it tick, and then challenge yourself to reassemble it. This experiment is a fantastic way to peek into engineering and see how innovation and improvement happen!

Concepts: Reverse engineering, dismantle, assemble

Material

🔩 *A small old toy, such as a pull-back toy car or a wind-up toy*

🔩 *A toolbox, including a set of screwdrivers*

Instructions

(1) Select an old toy that is not in use anymore but still functional, such as a pull-back toy car or a wind-up toy

(2) Play with the toy to learn what it does. Think of what mechanism allows the toy to work.

(3) Draw a diagram that illustrates how you imagine the toy looks like from inside and how the different parts work together

(4) Use a suitable screw driver and any other tools needed to dismantle the toy. Write down the steps you followed to dismantle it

(5) Inspect the toy from inside. Draw another diagram showing how the toy looks like from inside, including the parts you found

(6) Compare your initial diagram with the new one. Are they similar? What parts have you found that were not included in your initial diagram?

(7) Create a list and label it as "parts". Add the parts you found inside the toy with a brief description of what they do in the "parts" list

(8) After you develop an understanding of the parts, what they do, and how the toy works, think of ways to improve it

(9) Create a list and label it as "ideas to improve the existing design". Write down your ideas on how to improve the design of the toy

(10) The ideas to improve the design might include adding parts that would make the toy works better, or removing unnecessary parts

(11) Create a third list and label it as "New applications". Write down what new applications you can invent using the same mechanism of the toy

(12) Reassemble the toy by screwing the parts back together. Use the notes you took when you dismantled the toy to assemble the parts back

How it works

🔨 **Forward Engineering**: Involves constructing new systems or products from the ground up, starting with specific requirements.

📐 **Design and Implementation**: Engineers design, test, refine, and implement systems based on these requirements.

🔍 **Reverse Engineering**: Focuses on disassembling existing systems to understand their internal components and design.

🔧 **Rebuilding and Analysis**: Allows for rebuilding defective products, identifying weaknesses, and learning from current designs.

💡 **Innovation Through Reverse Engineering**: Engineers use insights from reverse engineering for developing new products and innovations.

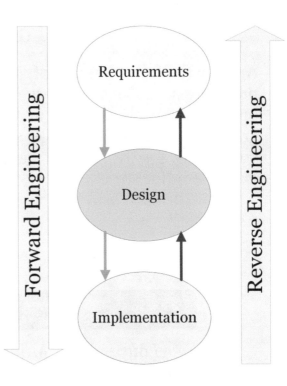

(25) Explore Your Engineering Intrest

Are you curious about which area of engineering captivates you the most? The field of engineering is vast and diverse, encompassing everything from groundbreaking inventions to the application of complex scientific principles. Whether it's mechanical, electrical, civil, or environmental engineering, each branch plays a pivotal role in shaping our world and enhancing our quality of life. Through this engaging activity, you'll delve into your own interests and preferences, uncovering which engineering discipline truly resonates with you. Get ready to unlock your potential and find your passion in the world of engineering!

Instructions

Answer the following sets of questions on a scale from 0 to 10. Use 0 for no interest and 10 for a very strong interest. Fill in your interest rating opposite to each question and sum up the total interest score for each group. During the test, make sure to eliminate any disturbances around you. Your answer should reflect your genuine interest without any external influences.

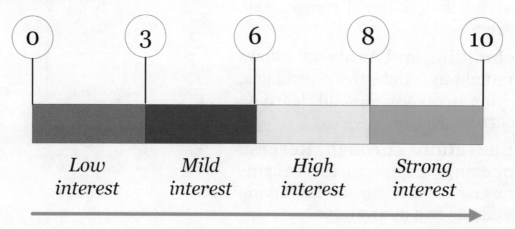

| 0 | 3 | 6 | 8 | 10 |

Low interest   *Mild interest*   *High interest*   *Strong interest*

Group A

	Question	Interest (From 0 to 10)
(1)	Do you like to dismantle a toy to figure out how it works?	
(2)	Do you like flying a drone?	
(3)	Do you like playing with toys that contain springs and levers?	
(4)	Do you like exploring forces and movement?	
(5)	Are you curious about energy transformation, such as potential into kinetic energy?	
(6)	Are you curious about how fans and pumps work?	
	How interesting the following experiments were to you:	
(7)	**Experiment (1)**: Air-powered fast car	
(8)	**Experiment (3)**: Egyptian Screw Pump	
(9)	**Experiment (4)**: Turbo Glider	
(10)	**Experiment (13)**: Energy in a Bottle	
Overall interest score for Group A (Sum interests on the right column)		

Group B

	Question	Interest (From 0 to 10)
(1)	Are you curious about the wiring inside a drone or a remote-controlled car toy?	
(2)	Do you like to work on wires and light bulbs?	
(3)	Are you interested in looking inside a speaker and figuring out how it works?	
(4)	Would you like to work on designing a network for several computers?	
(5)	Are you curious about how a T.V. remote control works?	
(6)	Would you like to build a temperature or pressure sensor?	
(7)	Do you like activities that involve magnets?	
(8)	Would you like to dismantle a laptop and rewire it again?	
	How interesting the following experiments were to you:	
(9)	**Experiment (7)**: Nail Magnet	
(10)	**Experiment (9)**: Candle Carousel	
Overall interest score for Group B (Sum interests on the right column)		

Group C

	Question	Interest (From 0 to 10)
(1)	Do you like playing with different materials and checking their composition?	
(2)	Are you curious about how they manufacture medicines?	
(3)	Do you like to investigate how plants differ from each other?	
(4)	Would you like to learn about nanotechnology and how it is used?	
(5)	Are you curious why some materials are degradable, and others are not?	
(6)	Do you like to spend time taking water samples from a pond?	
	How interesting the following experiments were to you:	
(7)	**Experiment (10)**: Colourful Flower	
(8)	**Experiment (15)**: Acid Rain in a Jar	
(9)	**Experiment (17)**: Cabbage Liquid Indicator	
(10)	**Experiment (19)**: Milk Star-shaped Plastic	
Overall interest score for Group C (Sum interests on the right column)		

Group D

	Question	Interest (From 0 to 10)
(1)	Do you like to design roads, such as highways, bridges, and traffic lights?	
(2)	Do you like to build structures using Lego blocks?	
(3)	Are you curious to know where wastewater goes and how it gets recycled?	
(4)	Would you like to build an instrument that reduces air pollution?	
(5)	Would you like to install solar cells on your home roof or backyard?	
(6)	Are you interested in generating electricity from water (hydropower)?	
	How interesting the following experiments were to you:	
(7)	**Experiment (12)**: Sunset in a Jar	
(8)	**Experiment (13)**: Energy in a Bottle	
(9)	**Experiment (14)**: Climate Change in a Jar	
(10)	**Experiment (15)**: Acid Rain in a Jar	
Overall interest score for Group D (Sum interests on the right column)		

Test Results

If your interest score was the highest for **Group A**, you could become a **Mechanical / Aerospace Engineer**!

Mechanical Engineering Scope: Involves working with material properties, heat transfer, and movement of gases and fluids.

Aerospace Engineering Focus: Specializes in control applications and systems in the aerospace sector.

Versatile Career Paths: Opportunities in power and energy, aerospace industry, automotive sector, product design, and manufacturing.

If your interest score was the highest for **Group B**, you could become an **Electrical / Electronic Engineer**!

Electrical Engineering Focus: Involves power systems, digital and analog electronics, signal processing, and telecommunications.

Diverse Career Options: Opportunities in power generation and distribution, construction projects, automotive and aerospace industries.

Electronics Specialization: Involves working in electronics design and manufacturing.

Space Exploration and Robotics: Opportunities to work in cutting-edge fields like space technology and robotics, using electrical/electronic engineering principles.

If your interest score was the highest for **Group C**, you could become a **Chemical / Biological Engineer!**

🖊 **Chemical and Biological Engineering Focus**: Involves chemical processes, petrochemicals, nanotechnology, product quality control, and materials properties.

🏷 **Pharmaceutical Industry**: Opportunities for chemical engineers to work in drug development and manufacturing.

🏭 **Manufacturing Plants**: Involvement in the production and quality control of various products.

⛽ **Oil and Gas Industry**: Engaging in petrochemical processing and energy production.

If your interest score was the highest for **Group D**, you could become a **Civil / Environmental Engineer!**

🏗 **Civil and Environmental Engineering**: Focuses on the built environment, including constructing structures like houses and buildings.

🌃 **Transportation Infrastructure**: Involves engineering aspects of transportation systems.

🌱 **Environmental Science Emphasis**: Addresses aspects of environmental protection and sustainability.

🔋 **Renewable Energy Resources**: Engages in the development and management of sustainable energy sources.

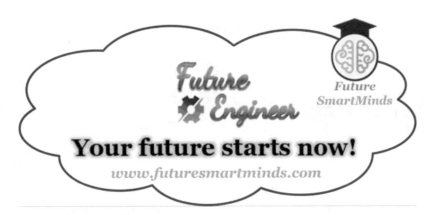

Your future starts now!

www.futuresmartminds.com

Thank you for choosing "**Future Engineer**" from our **STEM Explorers Series: Ignite the Future**. We sincerely hope that you and your young explorers have embarked on a fruitful learning experience, discovering the wonders of Engineering together. Your journey into inquiry and discovery is truly invaluable, and we are delighted to have been a part of it.

Your feedback is invaluable to us. If "**Future Engineer**" has kindled the spirit of innovation in your young engineer or brought educational joy to your family, please consider sharing your thoughts on Amazon. Your review will help other parents and aspiring engineers explore the wonders within these pages.

Scan to Rate Us on Amazon

We invite you and your aspiring learner to continue this enriching journey with the other titles in our series. Each book is crafted to open up new horizons of knowledge and imagination:

⚙ "**Future Scientist**" for a hands-on exploration into the world of Science,

🔢 "**Future Mathematician**" to unlock the intriguing puzzles of mathematics,

🔍 "**Future Chef**" to blend the art of cooking with scientific discovery,

🤖 "**Future AI Expert**" to step into the realm of artificial intelligence.

Every book is an opportunity to ignite a lifelong passion for learning and discovery. We can't wait to see where your next adventure takes you!

With warm regards,

www.futuresmartminds.com

Please check our other kids' **STEM** activities books!

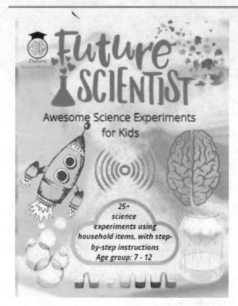

Available on Amazon!

(Scan the QR code to visit Amazon store)

Prepare for an exciting journey into the world of science! Our book is designed to captivate young minds, ages 7 to 12, with engaging experiments that uncover the magic of scientific concepts. These experiments unravel unpredictable phenomena, demonstrating that science explains the unexplained.

Unlock the World of Science: Science is all around us, and we've crafted mind-blowing experiments using everyday household items to demystify its wonders. These activities nurture analytical skills, critical thinking, and curiosity in physics, biology, chemistry, space, and technology.

Available on Amazon!

(Scan the QR code to visit Amazon store)

Prepare your child for an exciting mathematical journey with **"Future Mathematician."** This extraordinary book is specially crafted for young minds, ages 7 to 12, making mathematics not just accessible but enjoyable, empowering them with the skills they need to tackle real-world math challenges.

Unlocking Mathematical Magic: Mathematics is everywhere around us, but sometimes it can seem disconnected from our daily lives. **"Future Mathematician"** breaks down these barriers, revealing the enchanting world of math that surrounds us every day. This book bridges the gap between the classroom and reality, showing kids the profound importance of math in their lives.

Please check our other kids' **STEM** activities books!

Unleash Your Child's Potential with Artificial Intelligence (AI)! "**Future AI Expert**," where the wonders of artificial intelligence unfold through 20 captivating activities. Designed for young minds aged 7-12, this book offers a thrilling introduction to AI, blending education with a whole lot of interactive fun.

20 Amazing AI Activities: Engage with a variety of projects, from AI-powered storytelling to problem-solving games, each designed to spark curiosity and encourage exploration.

Easy to Follow, Fun to Learn: With kid-friendly instructions, the complex world of AI becomes an exciting playground for young minds.

Prepare to embark on an exciting journey where the joy of **cooking** meets the wonder of **science**! This vibrant cookbook is packed with **25 delicious cooking experiments** crafted for young chefs, aged 7 to 12, offering diverse hands-on experiments across five captivating sections: Bake, Grill, Boil, Fry, and Desserts.

Interactive Learning Experience: With step-by-step instructions, ingredient lists, and required equipment for each cooking experiment, **'Future Chef'** transforms the kitchen into a vivid laboratory. Through vibrant illustrations, scientific principles come alive, ensuring that each recipe is an engaging exploration of culinary science.

Made in United States
Cleveland, OH
29 December 2024

12820063R00044